JESSIE SCHUT

I BELIEVE

GETTING READY TO PROFESS MY FAITH

FAITH
ALIVE®
Christian Resources

Grand Rapids, Michigan

Faith Alive Christian Resources published by CRC Publications.
I Believe: Getting Ready to Profess My Faith © 2004, CRC Publications, 2850 Kalamazoo Ave. SE, Grand Rapids, MI 49560. All rights reserved. With the exception of brief excerpts for review purposes, no part of this book may be reproduced in any manner whatsoever without written permission from the publisher. Printed in the United States of America on recycled paper.

We welcome your comments. Call us at 1-800-333-8300 or e-mail us at editors@faithaliveresources.org.

ISBN 1-56212-978-3

10 9 8 7 6 5 4 3 2 1

CONTENTS

You've read the Bible, heard the stories, been part of a congregation. You've prayed and confessed your sins to Jesus. You believe in your heart that he is your Savior and Lord. Then one day you decided you wanted to tell the world: I believe! You asked your church leaders about professing your faith, and they've asked you to take this course called *I Believe*. What's it all about?

This is a program where you and one other person will sit down for eight sessions to figure out what you do believe and what it will mean for the rest of your life. (If you're taking this course as part of a small group or class, ignore the comments about mentoring that follow.) This other person, an adult, is a mentor. You are called a mentee—OK, it's a weird name but there really isn't any other word for it!

Mentors and mentees have been around a long time. The first mentor was a person named Mentor! He is mentioned in a book written by Homer thousands of years ago. In the story, Odysseus, a Greek warrior, is heading off to war, and he appoints a guy named Mentor to watch over his son Telemachus while he is gone, to be his teacher, guide, and friend.

So a mentor is someone who agrees to walk alongside another person as that person learns and grows. A mentor is someone who will listen and answer questions, who will be a friend and support you as you figure things out for yourself.

Here are some FAQs to help you learn more about *I Believe:*

1. WHAT WILL HAPPEN DURING THIS COURSE?

- You'll meet with your mentor once a week for eight weeks.
- You'll talk about the topic of the week and work through questions about it in this notebook.
- You'll work on your own "holy habits:" daily Bible reading and prayer.
- You'll create a personal expression of what you believe: something that will tell your congregation about your faith. It could be a written statement, a

song, a piece of art, a dance. It will be your own—nobody else can do this for you.

- You'll decide whether you wish to make profession of faith. If you do, you and your mentor will meet with your church leaders to tell them so. Then you'll participate in a ceremony to celebrate your profession.
- Other things might also happen. You might sit together with your mentor in church and discuss the service afterward. You might get together with your mentor on a social visit. You might decide to do a service project together. Those are all decisions you and your mentor can talk about once you've gotten together.

2. WHAT DO I HAVE TO DO IN THIS COURSE?

You will be asked to commit to

- meeting with your mentor for eight sessions.
- completing the work in this *I Believe* notebook.
- creating your own personal expression of faith.
- being sincere about exploring and thinking about your faith.
- being honest with your mentor.

At your first meeting, you and your mentor will talk about these commitments, and you and your mentor will both sign a covenant—a promise that tells what you have agreed to do.

3. WHAT'S MY MENTOR'S JOB?

Your mentor will commit to

- meeting with you for eight sessions.
- completing the work in his or her copy of this notebook.
- creating a personal statement of faith.
- being sincere about helping you explore your faith.
- praying for you regularly.
- being the best kind of mentor God has given him or her the gifts to be.

As you can see, a mentor is learning and growing along with you. You may ask your mentor questions, share concerns and problems, talk about your doubts and fears, and ask for advice.

4. WHAT HAPPENS IF I DON'T GET ALONG WITH MY MENTOR?

Remember, mentors are volunteers who sincerely want to be your friend. Your church wants to make this a great experience for you, so they've tried their best to match you with someone they think will be a good fit.

But sometimes, especially if you and your mentor are complete strangers to each other, you just don't click. There are a number of things you can do if you aren't connecting:

First, pray about it. Ask the Lord to give you ideas about how to improve the relationship. Second, if there is something specific that your mentor is doing that bothers you, talk about it. You might say something like, "When I tell you something, you sometimes interrupt me," or, "It seems to me you don't think my problems are very important." It takes a lot of courage to do this; sometimes, writing down your concerns in an e-mail may be easier than saying it in person. Third, discuss the situation with a parent or other adult you trust, asking for advice. Sometimes they may be able to help you see a different side of the problem.

Last, talk to your church leadership (pastor, youth leader), asking if they will step in and help. They may hook you up with a different mentor.

5. I'M REALLY, REALLY BUSY ALL THE TIME. I MIGHT NOT HAVE TIME TO READ THE BIBLE OR PRAY, OR CREATE MY PERSONAL STATEMENT OF FAITH. WHAT SHOULD I DO IF I CAN'T FIND TIME TO DO THE ASSIGNMENTS?

Life can be crazy busy, it's true—homework, sports, music lessons, friends, chores, school projects, part-time jobs, youth group outings, TV, the Internet, and video games all take time. And now, with *I Believe,* you've got a new commitment. Can you do it all?

Maybe not. You have to decide what's most important in your life. If you believe it is important to spend time on your walk with God, you will have to make time for it. Maybe you will have to drop something else that's less important, like TV or video games. Maybe you'll have to spend a little less time with your friends, or listening to your favorite music.

When you really think about it, is there anything more important than God and your relationship with him? Make time—you'll be glad you did.

6. CAN YOU GIVE ME SOME IDEAS ABOUT HOW I SHOULD CREATE MY PERSONAL "I BELIEVE" STATEMENT?

A statement of beliefs is called a "creed." For many years, the church has recited the Apostles' Creed. It's a statement of what the church believes, composed of words, sentences, and ideas. That's one kind of creed—spoken and written. You may wish to write your own series of statements about your beliefs about God, Jesus, the Holy Spirit, the church, and so on. This notebook has an "I Believe" section (starting with session 2) that will help you write your own statement of faith.

There are also songs that express a creed. Your church's hymnal may have such songs. A singer named Rich Mullins wrote a song based on the Apostles' Creed called "Creed." (You can hear it on the CD *Offerings II* by Third Day—see the words on the next page.) Other singers have done their own songs, each of them thinking about what they believe and writing it down in a song. So writing your own song is another way of expressing your beliefs.

Other people with God's gift of creative arts have expressed their creed in beautiful artworks that tell the world about their beliefs about God the Father, Jesus Christ, and the Holy Spirit. If you enjoy drawing or sculpting, you could express your beliefs by creating a piece of art. Or if you enjoy movement, liturgical dance is another way you could express your faith.

Often, symbols can express big ideas. For instance, the cross is a symbol of Christ's salvation; the dove is a symbol of the Holy Spirit; and the light of a candle can symbolize Christ as the light of the world. Your personal creed could be a banner that uses symbols to express what you believe. If you choose this to express your faith, you could write an explanation of your banner to accompany it.

There are many ways to create your own creed. Talk it over with your mentor at the first session. Do a little at a time and work on it week by week—you'll be using your gifts. You may also be asked to share your creed with the church during your profession of faith. That's a good thing—your gifts will help God's people to grow and celebrate.

CREED

I believe in God the Father
Almighty Maker of Heaven and Maker of Earth
And in Jesus Christ His only begotten Son, our Lord
He was conceived by the Holy Spirit
Born of the virgin Mary
Suffered under Pontius Pilate
He was crucified and dead and buried
And I believe what I believe is what makes me what I am
I did not make it, no it is making me
It is the very truth of God and not the invention of any man
I believe that He who suffered was crucified, buried, and dead
He descended into hell and on the third day, rose again
He ascended into Heaven where He sits at God's mighty right hand
I believe that He's returning
To judge the quick and the dead of the sons of men
And I believe what I believe is what makes me what I am
I did not make it, no it is making me
It is the very truth of God and not the invention of any man
I believe it, I believe it
I believe it
I believe it, I believe it
I believe in God the Father
Almighty Maker of Heaven and Maker of Earth
And in Jesus Christ His only begotten Son, our Lord
I believe in the Holy Spirit
One Holy Church
The communion of Saints
The forgiveness of sin
I believe in the resurrection
I believe in a life that never ends
And I believe what I believe is what makes me what I am
I did not make it, no it is making me
I did not make it, no it is making me
I said I did not make it, no it is making me
It is the very truth of God and not the invention of any man
I believe it, I believe
I believe it, I believe
I believe it, I believe it
I believe it, I believe it
I believe it, I believe it
I believe it

Words: Rich Mullins

7. CAN I "FAIL" THIS COURSE?

There is no test at the end of this course to see if you have "passed" your profession of faith. You won't get graded or have a report card to show your family. Church leaders will not check your notebook to make sure you know all the right stuff. So no, you can't "fail" this course.

If you are sincere about professing your faith, understand what it means, do your best to complete the assignments, and keep your appointments for meetings (unless you have a good reason for missing and let your mentor know ahead of time) your church will joyfully invite you to meet with its leaders to share your personal testimony, and welcome you to a celebration of your profession of faith.

However, it's also possible that these things might happen:

■ You might say, "I would like more time to think and pray and study before I make profession of faith." That's not failing. That's admitting you are not yet ready to take this step.

■ On rare occasions your mentor might say, "I'm not sure that my mentee really understands what she believes. I hope she'll spend a little more time thinking about this before she does profession of faith." And that's not failing either. Someone who cares about you and wants the best for you is helping you not settle for second best.

Anyone who takes the time to study God's Word and to think about their faith and their place in God's world is loved and accepted in God's eyes.

8. WHAT HAPPENS AT THE END OF THIS COURSE?

Your church leaders will meet with you and you will participate in a ceremony to profess your faith.

Every church has different traditions for this celebration. Perhaps your mentor and your parents will be asked to participate in the ceremony. Perhaps you will have a chance to share and talk about your personal statement of faith. Perhaps the church leaders will present you with a devotional book or invite you to make a public commitment to a ministry in the church. Whatever happens, it will be a great celebration.

However, just because you have made profession of faith does not mean that you are all done learning about your faith, the Bible, and the church. Christians never stop growing. You should continue to attend church education classes, worship with your congregation, and get involved in serving God. All of these things help you grow in your faith.

And someday, hopefully, someone may ask you to become a mentor. You'll remember how your mentor helped you better understand what faith was all about. And we hope you'll say, "I believe . . . and I'd love to help others grow too." That's what this course is all about!

DO . . .

- be honest with your mentor.
- keep your appointments for your meetings (or let your mentor know if you have a good reason for not keeping it).
- complete your assignments.
- be willing to grow and change.
- share your experiences with your parents and friends.
- ask questions (no question is a stupid question!).
- pray for your mentor, yourself, and your church.
- be yourself.
- think about and express what you—not your parents, teachers, friends, siblings or anyone else—believe.
- be a good listener.

DON'T . . .

- be afraid . . . remember, you're walking with God.
- keep your doubts inside.
- try to cram your assignments into one evening's work.

That's it! Be sure to ask your mentor if you have other questions we haven't answered. And enjoy your time together.

GOALS

- Get acquainted with my mentor and this program.
- Begin a personal timeline.
- Commit to completing this course with my mentor.
- Begin practicing "holy habits" at home this week.

I BELIEVE

PERSONALITY PLUS

Circle five words in each column that best describe you.

Weaknesses
- 🔊 Restless
- 👁 Selfish
- ▦ Inconsiderate
- ♟ Negative
- 👁 Stingy
- 🔊 Weak-willed
- ▦ Bossy
- ♟ Impractical
- 👁 Slow
- ▦ Hot-tempered
- 🔊 Loud
- ♟ Self-Centered
- 👁 Teaser
- ▦ Cruel
- 🔊 Impulsive
- ♟ Critical
- ▦ Proud
- 🔊 Exaggerates
- ♟ Stubborn
- 👁 Lazy

Strengths
- 🔊 Outgoing
- 👁 Calm
- ♟ Loyal
- ▦ Confident
- 👁 Productive
- ♟ Sensitive
- 🔊 Talkative
- ▦ Strong-willed
- ♟ Gifted
- 🔊 Carefree
- ♟ Perfectionist
- 👁 Humorous
- 🔊 Warm
- ▦ Practical
- 👁 Dependable
- ▦ Leader
- 👁 Easygoing
- ♟ Idealistic
- 🔊 Enthusiastic
- ▦ Independent

Count up your scores:

🔊:

▦:

👁:

♟:

14

This simple personality test can't begin to tell everything about you, so don't take it too seriously. However, you will likely score more highly in one category than in the other three. Here's what your highest score suggests about you:

🔊: You are fun-loving, enjoy being with people, enthusiastic, and energetic.

💾: You are quick to act, determined, practical, and like to organize things.

👁: You are easygoing, like to please others, consistent, and a good listener.

🌿: You are creative, faithful to your friends, dependable, and don't like to be in the limelight.

—adapted from *Successful Youth Mentoring,* Group Publishing, Inc.
© 1998, pages 32-33.

WHICH WOULD YOU RATHER DO?

If you had two choices, which of these would you rather do? Circle your choice, then compare with your partner. Are you more alike or different?

A. read a good book **OR** go for a run

B. get together with your friends **OR** watch a video at home

C. have a hamburger and fries **OR** have a veggie stir fry with rice

D. play video games **OR** play a sport

E. sing **OR** paint

F. go camping **OR** stay in a fancy hotel

MY FAVORITE . . .

Music: _____

Book: _____

Movie: _____

Game: _____

Color: _____

If I could be any animal I wanted to be, I would be a _____

because _____

WORLD AND PERSONAL TIMELINES

First movie with sound.

Germany defeats Denmark, Belgium, Holland, France; England declares war on Germany.

Rosa Parks arrested for sitting in bus seat reserved for whites; polio vaccine discovered; Disneyland opens in Los Angeles.

First man on the moon.

Donald Duck created; Monopoly invented.

First atomic bomb falls, ending World War II; first digital computer invented.

Martin Luther King jailed for civil rights march; Russian astronaut takes first walk in space; first snowboard invented.

End of Vietnam War.

| 1924 | 1927 | 1930 | 1934 | 1939 | 1940 | 1941 | 1945 | 1950 | 1955 | 1960 | 1965 | 1968 | 1969 | 1970 | 1975 |

Celluwipes— now known as Kleenex—hit the market.

Hitler invades Poland and Czechoslovakia.

Korean War begins; first transcontinental TV broadcast; first jet service from London to Paris.

Martin Luther King killed.

IBM ma first pers com

Plastic invented; first analog computer.

Japan bombs Pearl Harbor —U.S. enters the war.

First felt-tip pen sold; JFK becomes youngest president of U.S.

First Earth Da celebrated; IE introduces floppy disks the compute

PERSONAL TIMELINE

t St. Helens s in ington; e Strikes hits big n; AIDS nosed.

Soviet Union collapses; Iraq loses Gulf War; typhoon kills 139,000 people in Bangladesh— 10 million homeless.

First World Trade Center bombing; *Jurassic Park* makes most money ever; war in Bosnia.

Earthquake in Kobe, Japan, kills 2,700 people; *ER* top TV show.

Princess Diana dies in a car crash; Mother Teresa dies; *Harry Potter and the Sorcerer's Stone* published.

Michael Jordan retires for the second time; *Who Wants to Be a Millionaire* is top TV show.

September 11: terrorists destroy World Trade Center Towers and part of Pentagon, over 3,000 die; U.S. and allies invade Afghanistan.

U.S. invades Iraq; space shuttle Columbia explodes, killing 7; massive power blackout hits major eastern U.S. and Canadian cities.

Nuclear atastrophe at Chernobyl.

| 1985 | 1989 | 1990 | 1991 | 1992 | 1993 | 1994 | 1995 | 1996 | 1997 | 1998 | 1999 | 2000 | 2001 | 2002 | 2003 |

Hubble space telescope launched into space; Iraq invades Kuwait; Nintendo creates Game Boy.

Nelson Mandela becomes first black president of South Africa; tunnel opens between England and France; slaughter in Rwanda kills millions of people; Cal Ripkin sets record of 2,130 baseball games.

Fossil dinosaur bones bigger than Tyrannosaurus Rex found in Sahara Desert; 100th Olympic Games held in Atlanta, Georgia.

Hurricane Mitch kills 10,000 people in Central America.

al Qaeda hunted in Afghanistan caves; Bin Laden escapes.

AIDS declared an epidemic.

Los Angeles race riots; first UN Earth Summit meets in Rio de Janeiro.

New millennium! Y2K computer bug fails to cause predicted wipeouts.

- What was happening in the world when you were born?
- What was happening in the world when your parents were born? Your grandparents?
- What world events have had an impact on your life?
- On your personal timeline, mark important events in your life. Label them in the space **above** the line. For instance: the date of your birth; arrival of siblings; moves from one home to another; arrival of pets; graduations; achieving goals in sports, music, school.
- The space **below** the personal timeline is for important milestones on your faith journey. If you can fill in some of those, do so now. For instance: when you were baptized; when you first remember thinking about God; a special time when God answered your prayer or you felt very close to God; a hard time when you wondered why something happened or you doubted your faith; when you decided you would like to make profession of faith.

COVENANT

This *I Believe* course asks you to make a commitment to get ready for making profession of faith. Read through this covenant (promise) and sign it to show that you understand what your commitment is.

A covenant of commitment

between _____ and _____.

We promise to
- meet together once a week for eight weeks.
- complete the work in the *I Believe* notebook.
- be sincere about exploring and thinking about our faith.
- pray for one another regularly.

We will try to meet at a regular time and place:

_____.

If an unexpected event interferes with this plan, we will tell each other and make plans for another date. I can contact my partner at:

_____.

Together, we will try to reach these goals:

Other details:

Signed: _____

and _____

Date: _____

BIBLE READING FOR THE WEEK

"Holy habits" help Christians grow. Prayer and Bible reading are two very important holy habits. Choose five days out of the next seven to read a Bible passage; answer the question after each passage, or just write down your own ideas, then pray.

Day 1: Read Luke 2:41-52.
Jesus grew in wisdom and stature. In what ways would you like to grow?

Day 2: Read 1 Timothy 4:8-12.
How does your church show (or not show) that it values your faith?

Day 3: Read Psalm 119:97-105.
How can God's Word help keep you on the right path?

Day 4: Read Colossians 3:12-17.
How can God's people help keep you on the right path?

Day 5: Read 1 Corinthians 13.
How does love keep you on the right path?

PRAYER PATTERNS

For your prayer time each day this week, try using a style called ACTS: Adoration, Confession, Thanksgiving, and Supplication. Many Christians find that praying this way helps them focus.

- **Adoration** (I worship you, Lord, for . . .)
- **Confession** (I'm sorry, Lord, for . . .)
- **Thanksgiving** (Thank you, Lord, for . . .)
- **Supplication** (I ask you, Lord, for . . .)

In the "supplication" part of your prayer, please pray for your mentor (as he or she will pray for you), and pray that God will bless the time you spend together. Believe that God will honor your request and use your relationship with your mentor to prepare you for professing your faith.

GOALS

- Explore what I know, think, and feel about God.
- Discover what the Bible has to say about God.
- Learn what the church believes about God.
- Write down what I believe about God.

I BELIEVE

WHAT DO YOU KNOW ABOUT GOD?

Mark the place on the graph where you think you fit.

I know lots about God.

I know practically nothing about God.

PICTURES OF GOD

How did you think about God when you were a little child? What did you imagine God looked like? Draw a picture in the box.

How has your picture of God changed over the years? Draw a picture of what you imagine God might look like now.

OTHER WAYS OF EXPERIENCING GOD

If You Were a Musician . . .

what instruments would you feature in a song that describes God?

- soft-strumming guitar solo
- wild drumming and percussion
- rousing trumpet fanfare
- deep rumbling pipe organ
- loud, attention-getting heavy metal rock
- a whole orchestra playing in perfect hamony
- other: _____

If You Were an Artist . . .

what colors would you feature in a picture that expresses what God means to you?

- bright reds, yellows, and blues
- soft pastel colors
- stark black and white
- all the colors I could think of
- all the shades of my favorite color
- earth tones of green, brown, and gold
- brilliant gold
- other: _____

What shapes would you use in your picture of God?

- lots of circles
- flame shapes
- triangles, squares, rectangles
- irregular shapes, wavy lines
- many straight lines
- other: _____

When or where have you recently felt close to God?

- with my family
- in church
- alone in my room
- while on a service project
- while reading the Bible or praying
- while enjoying nature
- other: _____

WHAT THE BIBLE SAYS ABOUT GOD

The Bible has many images of God. Almost every page tells something about God. But even the Bible isn't big enough to hold a complete view of God. We won't know the whole truth until we meet God in heaven!

In the meantime, since we're not exactly in heaven yet, use these passages to list a few of the Bible's many names and descriptions of God. Which seems the most real to you? Which would you like to experience more?

■ Deuteronomy 32:4

■ Isaiah 28:29

■ Psalm 19:1

■ Psalm 23:1

■ Psalm 147:3

■ Proverbs 18:10

■ Isaiah 43:15

■ Isaiah 66:13

■ Isaiah 64:8

■ John 3:16

■ 1 John 3:1

■ Deuteronomy 32:11

What does it mean to you that you have been made in the image of God?

WHAT THE CHURCH BELIEVES ABOUT GOD

Through the ages, God's people have tried to put into words what Christians believed. They did this so that people could understand what the Bible teaches. Also, they did it so that they would have a standard against which to measure false beliefs. These statements of beliefs are called "creeds" (from the Latin word *credo* meaning "I believe").

Here are examples of what some creeds say about God:

- I believe in God the Father Almighty, maker of heaven and earth . . . (Apostles' Creed, one of the best-known confessions of churches around the world).
- We believe in the one God, maker and ruler of all things, Father of all men, and the source of all goodness and beauty, all truth and love . . . (Korean Creed, adopted by the Methodist church in Korea in 1930).
- I believe in God, who created woman and man in God's own image, who created the world and gave both sexes the care of the earth . . . (A Woman's Creed, written in 1983 for a women's gathering at the World Council of Churches).
- Our world belongs to God—not to us or earthly powers, not to demons, fate, or chance. The earth is the Lord's! (*Our World Belongs to God,* a Contemporary Testimony of the Christian Reformed Church).

I BELIEVE . . .

One of your commitments in this course is to write your own "I believe . . ." statement that tells what you believe. You can start this now by writing down what you believe about God:

Begin thinking about how you will express your personal statement of faith to the church when you do your profession of faith. Will you use words (as you've just done above) or pictures, a banner, photographs, dance, song or music? God has given each of his children special gifts. Use yours to help the church celebrate your profession.

HOLY HABITS

Day 1: Read Zephaniah 3:14-17.
Have you ever thought of God rejoicing over you with singing? How does that make you feel?

Day 2: Read Jeremiah 18:1-6.
Has God had to remold and reshape you at times? Describe such a time.

Day 3: Read Psalm 61:1-5.
When have you had to run to God for safety? Write a thank-you note to God for his protection.

Day 4: Read Psalm 103:8-14.
Think about some of the sins God has forgiven you for. Say a prayer of thanks to God for his grace and love.

Day 5: Read Revelation 21:1-5.
One day you will live with God! What are your feelings as you think about this?

PRAYER PATTERNS

If you enjoyed using the ACTS pattern of prayer, you may wish to continue that this week. However, if you want to do something different, you could try what's known as "intercessory prayer." An intercessor is someone who pleads on behalf of someone else. So intercessory prayer is prayer in which you regularly pray for the needs of another person.

Often, before you practice intercessory prayer, God prepares your heart. You notice that someone has needs, and you have a strong urge to pray for those needs. It might be a family member who's ill, a friend at school who doesn't know Jesus, someone whose parents are getting a divorce, a kid who's thinking about joining your youth group, the homeless who roam your downtown streets, war refugees in another land . . . the possibilities are endless.

Choose one or two people for whom you would like to become an intercessor. Pray every day for that person. Be specific, asking God to change the situation. Reflect on what God might want you to do. Perhaps you will want to enlist the help of a prayer partner who will remind you every day about your commitment.

P.S. Don't forget to continue interceding for the person who's mentoring you!

I BELIEVE . . . IN JESUS

GOALS

- Explore my ideas about Jesus.
- Explore the Bible's message that Jesus is Savior and Lord of the world.
- Affirm that I believe in Jesus as my personal Savior.
- Discover what the church believes about Jesus.
- Write down my personal beliefs about Jesus.

MY IDEAS ABOUT JESUS

Imagine that you are a well-known and gifted artist. You have been asked to paint a portrait of Jesus that captures for all Christians everywhere who the "real" Jesus is. What would you draw? Choose your own idea or select one of the following:

- An infant Jesus in his mother's arms.
- An angry Jesus driving the moneychangers from the temple.
- A laughing Jesus with little kids sitting on his lap.
- A compassionate Jesus healing the sick.
- A powerful Jesus calming the storm on the sea.
- A dying Jesus nailed to a cross.
- A victorious Jesus bursting out of the tomb.
- A triumphant Jesus ascending into heaven.
- A contemporary Jesus talking with a couple of kids at school.
- My own idea: _____

THE BIBLE'S PICTURE OF JESUS AS SAVIOR OF THE WORLD

Each Bible verse here is a piece of the big picture. Read and follow the instructions, starting with number 1 at the bottom of the page.

3. What does sin do?

Makes God seem _____. (Psalm 22:1)

Makes us feel _____. (Psalm 51:3-5)

Sin _____ us from God.

Draw a vertical barrier or gap between you and God.

Write the word "sin" on the barrier.

4. Who can bridge the gap between us and God?

John 3:16

John 14:6

Draw a bridge between you and God.

Write "Jesus" on the bridge.

GOD

2. What does God ask of us?

Love _____ and _____.

  (Matthew 22:37-39)

Be _____.

  (Leviticus 19:2)

Can we do this?

Draw a symbol to represent God under the word "God."

1. What's wrong with people?

When God made people, God said that they were very _____.

  (Genesis 1:31)

But Adam and Eve _____.

  (Genesis 3)

Now sin infects_____.

  (Romans 3:23)

Draw a picture of yourself under the word "you."

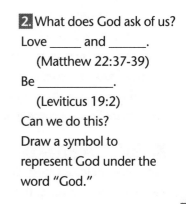

MY RESPONSE TO GOD'S GIFT OF SALVATION

Ask yourself these questions:

- Do you trust that Jesus' death and resurrection are for you?
- Do you accept God's gift of forgiveness?
- Is there any sin you may have done that's too big for God to forgive?
- Do you believe that God has made Jesus Lord of the whole world? What difference does that make in the way you live?
- How do you react to this good news? Use the space below to express your feelings and thoughts about Jesus' gift of salvation.

WHAT THE CHURCH BELIEVES ABOUT JESUS

APOSTLES' CREED

I believe . . . in Jesus Christ, his only begotten Son, our Lord,
who was conceived by the Holy Spirit
    and born of the virgin Mary.
He suffered under Pontius Pilate,
    was crucified, died, and was buried;
    he descended to hell.
The third day he rose again from the dead.
He ascended to heaven,
    and is seated at the right hand of God the Father almighty.
From there he shall come to judge the living and the dead. . . .

KOREAN CREED

We believe in Jesus Christ, God manifest in the flesh, our teacher, example, and Redeemer, the Savior of the world . . .

OUR WORLD BELONGS TO GOD

As our substitute,
[Jesus] suffered all his years on earth,
especially in the horrible torture of the cross.
He carried God's judgment on our sin;
his sacrifice removes our guilt.
He walked out of the grave, the Lord of life!
He conquered sin and death.
We are set right with God,
we are given new life,
and called to walk with him
in freedom from sin's dominion.

—stanza 27

EARLY CHURCH

In the early days of the church, Christians could not always say openly what they believed for fear of being persecuted and killed. They had to use a secret way to state their creed and let fellow Christians know that they were believers in Jesus. So they made or wore the shape of a fish. Each letter of the Greek word for fish *(ichthus)* stood for the first letter of the names the believers gave to Jesus: Jesus Christ, Son of God, Savior. This is what they believed; it was their creed.

Even today, people will let you know they believe in Jesus by the jewelry or clothes they wear: a WWJD bracelet, a cross on a chain, or a T-shirt with a Christian message. They are wearing their creed.

I BELIEVE . . .

This is what I believe about Jesus . . .

BIBLE READINGS FOR THE WEEK

This week's readings are things that Jesus said about himself.

Day 1: Read John 6:25-35.

Why do you think Jesus called himself "the bread of life"? What does this title tell you about Jesus?

Day 2: Read John 8:12.

Light banishes darkness and makes things clear. In what part of your life does Jesus' light need to shine?

Day 3: Read John 10:11-15.

How does knowing that Jesus is your "good shepherd" make you feel?

Day 4: Read John 14:5-11.

What does it mean to you that Jesus is "the way, the truth, and the life"?

Day 5: Read John 15:1-8.

Jesus says we are branches that bear fruit as long as we are attached to him (the Vine). What are you doing to stay attached to Jesus?

PRAYER PATTERNS

Here's a combination of written and spoken prayer that you may find helpful. At the beginning of the week, write (on small slips of paper) your personal concerns, prayer requests, and names of persons you want to intercede for. Every day draw out two or three slips of paper and pray for these concerns. Add more slips of paper to your stash as you go. On the back of the slips of paper, write down answers as they happen. Be sure to thank God for any requests that were granted.

GOALS

■ Talk about what I think the Holy Spirit is.

■ Learn about the work and person of the Holy Spirit according to the Bible.

■ Identify gifts that the Holy Spirit gives to the world and to me personally.

■ Discover what the church believes about the Holy Spirit.

■ Write down my beliefs about the Holy Spirit.

I BELIEVE

THE HOLY SPIRIT AT WORK

Which of the following do you think is the work of the Holy Spirit?

1. Eight Vietnamese villagers gather secretly in a home to study the Bible.
2. A big church in your town is turned into a recreation center.
3. The creation of the world.
4. A dozen churches of different denominations join together in a march for peace.
5. A woman forgives an arsonist who torched her home.
6. A simple young man becomes a leader of a nation.
7. You visit a lonely old lady who just moved in next door.

Write down an example of the work of the Holy Spirit that you have experienced personally.

WHAT BIBLE SAYS ABOUT THE HOLY SPIRIT

FROM THE DESK OF THE HOLY SPIRIT

Dear _____,

I hear that you wish to make profession of faith. Congratulations!

The Christian life is an exciting one. When you publicly profess your faith, you are inviting me to continue my work in your life. I'm excited about that!

Of course, I've been working in your life for a long time. I was there when you were born and baptized. I taught you truth. I was the voice of your conscience. And I prepared your heart for this day.

You may be wondering what plans I might have for you in the future—maybe it even sounds a little scary. So here's some information about me. Check it out for yourself. You'll see that you are in for exciting times when you let me get to work in your life. . . .

- I was present at creation (Genesis 1:2).
- I gave power to leaders such as Moses (Exodus 4:21) and Joshua (Deuteronomy 34:9). I turned weaklings into giants!
- I spoke to a boy and told him what God wanted him to do (1 Samuel 3:8-10).
- I inspired a shepherd boy to write beautiful songs that are still sung thousands of years later (Psalm 23).
- I helped a young slave girl save her master from leprosy (2 Kings 5:4).
- I filled an old man with supernatural power so he could race a chariot for miles and miles (1 Kings 18:45).
- I spoke to prophets like Isaiah and Ezekiel, and they passed God's words on to God's people.
- I was present when a very young person named Mary became pregnant with God's Son, Jesus (Matthew 1:18).
- I comforted Jesus' friends and filled them with supernatural abilities after Jesus went back to heaven (Acts 2:1-4).
- I brought many different people together to form the church (Acts 2:42-47).
- I helped Paul's young nephew save him from a plot to kill him (Acts 23:12-22).
- I helped spread the good news about Jesus from Jerusalem to Samaria, from Cyprus to Antioch, throughout Turkey and Greece, and on to Rome—all in only 60 years (the book of Acts).
- I have made millions of people believe in Jesus.

Your history books will tell about my work since then: how God's Word came to Europe, Asia, the Americas. Now Christianity has spread around the world.

But there is still work to do. Billions of people, including people right in your own neighborhood, still don't know or believe that Jesus is Savior and Lord of all. People are sad and hurting. Creation is suffering. Nations suffer through injustice and wars.

You are invited to help me speak God's words of love, forgiveness, and peace, to work for healing and justice. What do you say—shall we get on with it?

THE HOLY SPIRIT AND ME

SPIRITUAL GIFTS

You may wonder what you can do to help the work of God. God has given each of his children special gifts to do their work. Those are spiritual gifts. Find out what yours are, and work with the Holy Spirit to do the work of God!

- administration (organizing and helping people work together)

- leading (setting an example for others; helping them reach goals)

- prophesying (knowing God's Word and talking boldly about it)

- creative communications (music, art, writing, drama, dance, and so on)

- hospitality (making people feel comfortable, relaxed)

- teaching (clearly explaining things about God and how God wants us to live)

- discernment (telling if something is right or wrong, real or fake)

- faith (trusting God's promises, even in hard times)

- giving (cheerfully and generously sharing our time, money, and possessions)

- intercession (praying faithfully for others)

- mercy (sympathy for those who are hurt; helping them in meaningful ways)

- encouragement (using words/actions to cheer people up)

- evangelism (telling others about Jesus' love)

- service (helping others in practical ways)

- knowledge (understanding God's Word and how it relates to our lives)

BULLETIN BOARD

This is the place to jot down your questions and thoughts as you take this course. You'll have time during each session to share your thoughts with your mentor, who will be using a bulletin board too.

What could I do to help my church?

Sometimes I don't feel like praying. Should I skip it or just pray anyway?

Thanks, God, for a cool day at school!

IEVE

God, why do you allow bad things to happen?

Which of these gifts—or other gifts—do you think God may have given you? Ask your parents and other Christians who know you well if they agree with you.

Think about some ways you could use the gift or gifts the Holy Spirit has given you to serve God.

I could . . .

I could . . .

I could . . .

FRUIT OF THE SPIRIT (GALATIANS 5:22)

When the Holy Spirit lives in you, your life will be marked by the fruit of the Spirit. Pick three of these nine qualities and tell how you could show these qualities in your life this month.

PATIENCE

FAITHFULNESS

GENTLENESS

PEACE

LOVE

GOODNESS

SELF-CONTROL

KINDNESS

JOY

WHAT THE CHURCH BELIEVES ABOUT THE HOLY SPIRIT

THE APOSTLES' CREED

I believe in the Holy Spirit,
the holy catholic church,
    the communion of saints,
the forgiveness of sins,
the resurrection of the body,
and the life everlasting.

OUR WORLD BELONGS TO GOD

Jesus stays with us in the Spirit,
who renews our hearts,
moves us to faith,
leads us in the truth,
stands by us in our need,
and makes our obedience fresh and vibrant.
—stanza 31

The Spirit's gifts are here to stay
in rich variety—
fitting responses to timely needs.
We thankfully see each other
as gifted members of the fellowship
which delights in the creative Spirit's work.
He gives more than enough
to each believer
for God's praise and our neighbor's welfare.
—stanza 33

I BELIEVE . . .

What do you believe about the Holy Spirit?

BIBLE READINGS FOR THE WEEK

Day 1: Read Acts 2:1-4, 36-41.
How do you react to this story?

Day 2: Read Acts 2:42-47.
What is it about this picture that sounds good to you?

Day 3: Read Acts 7:54-8:3.
How was the Holy Spirit present here?

Day 4: Read Acts 11:19-30.
List all the ways you see the Holy Spirit working in these few verses.

Day 5: Read Acts 16:6-15.
List all the ways you see the Holy Spirit working in these verses.

PRAYER PATTERNS

This week, you may want to try using a journal for prayer. Writing down your prayers is one way to keep your attention focused on God.

Use a notebook with lots of blank pages, or, if you are used to writing at the computer, keep a file for your prayers. There is nothing unspiritual about praying at the computer with your eyes wide open!

Prayer beginnings may be hard. Here's an idea: begin each prayer with the words "Lord, today I . . ." Then tell the Lord about your day. What did you do? What made you excited? What made you sorry? What problems or highlights did you experience?

Often, writing out these events will bring to mind other things you want to talk to God about. You may want to confess a sin. You may remember that you need to pray for a friend who is going through tough times. You may want to ask God a question about something you did not understand—and you may want to discuss this question with your mentor at your next session.

Sometimes those blank pages may result in sketches or poems or jotting down a Scripture verse you want to think about. Prayer journals are great to read months or even years later. They remind you of things that God has done in your life, even though you may not have been aware of it at the time.

(Of course, if you are journaling your prayers early in the morning, you'd want to change that opening sentence to "Lord, yesterday I . . .".)

GOALS

- Think about what God asks of us.
- Describe how to make decisions that please God.
- Learn what the Bible and the church teach about doing good for God.
- Write my own beliefs about living a new life of service to God.

I BELIEVE

PLANET PERFECTA

Imagine someone has taken you to live on planet Perfecta, where everything is perfect. Write a description or draw a simple picture with labels to describe it.

Make a list of five important rules that govern planet Perfecta. For example, if your idea of a perfect planet includes clean air and water, you could have the rule "Factories and people are not allowed to pollute."

WHAT THE BIBLE SAYS

Once upon a time, planet Perfecta did exist. It was planet Earth. In the beginning, the rules God gave were very simple, and they were written on the hearts of the people, so they were easy to keep. But after planet Earth was ruined by sin, people thought they could do whatever they wished. So God gave ten basic rules or commandments to help people live the new life God provides for us through the Holy Spirit.

THE TEN COMMANDMENTS

Show love to God by obeying these commands:

1. Have no other gods.
2. Have no idols.
3. Don't misuse God's name.
4. Keep the Sabbath holy.

Show love to people by obeying these commands:

5. Honor father and mother.
6. Do not murder.
7. Do not commit adultery.
8. Do not steal.
9. Do not give false testimony.
10. Do not covet.

■ Compare your list for perfect living to God's list. Did you forget anything you'd like to add now?

God's rules can be summarized in just four words:

LOVE GOD.
LOVE OTHERS.

■ That sounds so simple! Is it?

MAKING CHOICES

Every day, you make choices: to ride your bike or walk, to order a burger or a taco, to lie or tell the truth. Some decisions are no-brainers; others can tie your stomach in knots and rob you of sleep.

It would be easy if you could just look up God's Big Ten—the Ten Commandments—and know exactly what to do. But it isn't always that simple. God's commands are general in nature. While they guide and inform our decisions, they're not meant to give quick and easy solutions to every difficulty we face. Sometimes one of God's commands may seem to conflict with another commandment in a specific situation. Sometimes entirely different solutions to a problem all seem to honor God's law equally.

Suppose you have to make a decision about choosing to go to youth group or attend a friend's party. God's commands won't tell you what to do. So how do you make up your mind?

Many Christians use these guidelines to help them make choices. Ask yourself . . .

■ **What does the Bible say?**

The Bible isn't a rule book, but its stories, songs, and teachings show us who God is and who we are. The Bible may not have direct advice about your problem, but it will help point you in the right direction.

■ **What does tradition say?**

Guess what? Other people have probably asked the same questions and faced the same problems you are now facing. You can often benefit from their insights. Your church may have appointed wise people to study issues that can help you in your decisions. The creeds and testimonies of your church can sometimes help you find answers to your questions about God and the Christian life.

■ **What does experience tell you?**

Have you faced this decision before? Sometimes making a wrong decision teaches us how to act in the future. And often, we can learn from other people's experiences (including that of your parents!).

■ **What does common sense tell you?**

God gave you a mind to think things through. The Holy Spirit can guide your thinking if you ask for wisdom. Talk to other people, gather information, and use it to make choices that are right for you and pleasing to God.

Some people like to make decisions based on their feelings, their friends' opinions, and what's politically correct.

WHAT WOULD YOU DO?

Read these situations and decide what you would do in each case. Use Scripture, tradition, experience, and common sense as your guidelines.

GOOD SAMARITAN

You're traveling alone on a lightly traveled road, heading to an interview for a job you're dying to get. It's a snowy morning and the roads are slick. You hold your speed down even though you're running a bit late. Suddenly, off to the right, you see taillights glowing upward at an impossible angle. You slow down, realizing that a car has skidded off the road into the ditch. From the road it's impossible to see if anyone is inside. Another driver passes you, impatiently laying on the horn. You wish you had your cell phone, but you left it home. Do you stop and investigate and risk being very late to the job interview, maybe ruining your chances (not to mention your good clothes)? Or do you drive on, thinking someone else will stop and be a good Samaritan?

—adapted from *No Easy Answers: Making Good Decisions in an Anything Goes World* (Faith Alive Christian Resources), page 123.

OLD FRIEND OR NEW FRIEND?

At last! You finally got an invitation to a Saturday-night party at Nadine's house. All year long you've heard about these parties but never been invited. Seems Nadine has finally chosen you to be part of her circle of friends. It sure feels good. Only problem, though, is your best friend. You've hung out with her for ages. Most every Saturday night you get together for a movie or a sleepover. And your friend didn't get an invite to Nadine's party. So how do you handle this? Do you say anything about the party to your friend? Say no to Nadine?

MONEY OR MISSION?

If you want to go to college, you know you're going to need to save a pile of money. You're not smart enough to get a great scholarship, and your family doesn't have the money to send you, especially after your baby brother was born with a rare medical condition that requires lots of expensive treatment. Your neighbor offers you a summer job babysitting so you can add to your college fund. But now your youth group has this amazing opportunity to go on a month-long mission trip doing clean-up at a Christian camp, helping with vacation Bible school, and cutting lawns for house-bound seniors. So what do you do? Stay home and make some much-needed money or go with your youth group on this exciting mission?

DAD OR MOM?

Not long ago, your dad found himself a new female friend, leaving you and your mom to fend for yourselves. The breakup's clearly his fault, at least as far as you can tell, and you're really mad at him. Now that the divorce has been finalized, your dad calls and says he wants to spend some time with you each week. You recall how little time he spent with you before the divorce—he was always gone at night, golfing with his friends on weekends, and he never attended any of your school functions. "I don't want you to see him," your mom says. "He doesn't deserve it." Part of you still loves your dad. So what do you do?

WHAT THE CHURCH SAYS

Q. How should you live as a Christian?

A. Thankful for God's salvation,
    I should live a new life
    of serving Christ, my Lord,
    every day in every way.

Q. How do you make this new life real?

A. By running away from sin
    and by trying eagerly to do every kind of good
    as God wants me to.

Q. What is this "good" God wants you to do?

A. Thoughts and actions which
    are done out of faith,
    agree with God's law,
    and praise God.
    —Q&A 50-52

OUR WORLD BELONGS TO GOD

We rejoice in the goodness of God,
renounce the works of darkness,
and dedicate ourselves to holy living.
As covenant partners,
called to faithful obedience,
and set free for joyful praise,
we offer our hearts and lives
to do God's work in his world. . . .
—stanza 6

I BELIEVE . . .

What do you believe about living a new life of serving God?

BIBLE READINGS FOR THE WEEK

This week's readings are New Testament versions of God's Big Ten. Jesus and the Holy Spirit teach us new ways of obeying God.

Day 1: Read Ephesians 4:22-5:21.

What part of your "old self" would you like to get rid of?

Day 2: Read 1 Thessalonians 5:5-11.

Mention one "command" or piece of advice in this passage and explain how it applies to your life.

Day 3: Read Matthew 5:1-12.

Do you know people who are examples of these descriptions (for example, someone who is merciful, someone who is a peacemaker)? Thank God for these people.

Day 4: Read Matthew 6:25-34.

What are you worried and upset about today? Can you trust God to take care of it?

Day 5: Read Matthew 25:31-46.

Do you know someone who needs your deeds of love and mercy? Ask God to show you what to do to help them. Then do it.

PRAYER PATTERNS

This week, you might like to try "prayer-walking."

Prayer-walking is very simple: you take a walk (or run or bike ride) and you ask God to bless the people in the houses and in the neighborhoods as you pass by. You can also pray for stores, businesses, and churches that you pass along the way.

Why do this? Because when you ask the Holy Spirit to be your guide, and when you are praying for people in your community, you are serving others with God's love. Some people you pray for may never have had anyone pray for them before. Some homes and businesses may be in trouble; your prayer shows you care.

And when you walk in a neighborhood, you will see very specific things that you may never have noticed before, for which you can pray: for example, a "For Sale" sign means you can pray for the family who is moving and for those who will buy the house; a fire hydrant reminds you to pray for those who work in fire protection; when you see city workers, you can pray for their safety.

Here are some things to consider before you decide to prayer-walk:

- Do not put yourself in an unsafe situation. If your community is unsafe to walk in alone, invite one or more adults to walk with you. Perhaps this is something your family can try for a week.
- Do not make a spectacle of yourself. You are not there to draw attention to yourself. You will be praying silently as you walk past people, residences, and businesses. You may want to take notes if you see something you'd like to pray more about, or do something about.
- Pray for the Holy Spirit's help; ask your mentor/mentee to pray for you too.

GOALS

- ■ Understand how worship and the sacraments can help me grow.
- ■ Affirm other specific ways the church can help me grow in my faith.
- ■ Learn about my church's commitment to me.
- ■ Write my own beliefs about the church and the sacraments.

I BELIEVE

GROWING IN MY FAITH

They are like a tree that is planted near a stream of water.
It always bears its fruit at the right time.
Its leaves don't dry up.
Everything godly people do turns out well.
—Psalm 1:3, NIrV

To grow well and produce good fruit, trees need fertile soil, proper nutrients, water, sunshine, protection from pests and frost, careful pruning, and other care.
■ What does the seed of faith need to grow well? List as many needs as you can think of.

■ How does the church help meet these needs?

The seed of faith in you has been planted and is growing. How would you describe that growth?

__ I'm a seedling—I need to grow a lot before I can bear fruit.
__ I'm just not getting enough nourishment to produce any fruit.
__ Right now I feel like I'm being attacked by these pests: _____.
__ I started growing really well but now I feel like nothing's happening.
__ I'm growing, and I can see some fruits of faith in my life.
__ Other: _____

WHAT THE BIBLE SAYS ABOUT WORSHIP

One way the church can help you grow spiritually is through worship. Highlight the words or phrases in these Bible verses that say something meaningful to you about worship.

"My soul gives glory to the Lord.
   My spirit delights in God my Savior.
He has taken note of me
even though I am not important.
From now on all people will call me blessed.
The Mighty One has done great things for me.
His name is holy.
He shows his mercy to those who have respect for him,
from parent to child down through the years."
—Mary's Song, Luke 1, NIrV

The LORD came and stood there, calling as at the other times, "Samuel! Samuel!" Then Samuel said, "Speak, for your servant is listening."
—1 Samuel 3:10

Guard your steps when you go to the house of God. Go near to listen rather than to offer the sacrifice of fools, who do not know that they do wrong. Do not be quick with your mouth, do not be hasty in your heart to utter anything before God. God is in heaven and you are on earth, so let your words be few.
—Ecclesiastes 5:7

I will praise you, O LORD, with all my heart;
I will tell of all your wonders.
I will be glad and rejoice in you;
I will sing praise to your name, O Most High.
—Psalm 9:1-2

They devoted themselves to the apostles' teaching and to the fellowship, to the breaking of bread and to prayer. Everyone was filled with awe, and many wonders and miraculous signs were done by the apostles. . . .
—Acts 2:42-43

"You are worthy, our Lord and God,
to receive glory and honor and power,
for you created all things. . . ."
—Revelation 4:11

How can the church help you worship God as best you can?

WHAT THE BIBLE SAYS ABOUT BAPTISM

OLD TESTAMENT

God told Abraham: "I will establish my covenant as an everlasting covenant between me and you and your descendants after you for the generations to come, to be your God and the God of your descendants after you" (Genesis 17:7).

■ The sign of this covenant was _____.

NEW TESTAMENT

Jesus made a new covenant with his people, a covenant of forgiveness. He told his disciples that his blood was "the blood of the covenant, which is poured out for many for the forgiveness of sins" (Matthew 26:28).

Jesus' disciples baptized many believers in this new covenant, both adults and children, saying, "The promise is for you and your children and for all whom the Lord our God will call" (Acts 2:39).

■ The sign of this covenant is _____.

■ Why is water a good sign for the sacrament of baptism?

■ If you've been baptized, what does your baptism mean to you? If you're planning to be baptized soon, what does this mean to you?

WHAT THE BIBLE SAYS ABOUT THE LORD'S SUPPER

OLD TESTAMENT

The Israelites celebrated the Passover Feast (or the Feast of Unleavened Bread), which was a remembrance of how God saved his people from the Egyptians.

"And when your children ask you, 'What does this ceremony mean to you?' then tell them, 'It is the Passover sacrifice to the LORD, who passed over the houses of the Israelites in Egypt and spared our homes when he struck down the Egyptians.' Then the people bowed down and worshiped."

—Exodus 12:26-27

NEW TESTAMENT

When Jesus came, he showed us a new way to celebrate: a supper to remember that our sins are forgiven through his blood.

"The Lord Jesus, on the night he was betrayed, took bread, and when he had given thanks, he broke it and said, 'This is my body, which is for you; do this in remembrance of me.' In the same way, after supper he took the cup, saying, 'This cup is the new covenant in my blood; do this, whenever you drink it, in remembrance of me.' For whenever you eat this bread and drink this cup, you proclaim the Lord's death until he comes."

—1 Corinthians 11:23-26

■ Why did Jesus tell us to celebrate his death often?

■ What does the Lord's Supper mean to you ?

THE HEIDELBERG CATECHISM

54. Q. What do you believe concerning "the holy catholic church"?

  A. I believe that the Son of God
      through his Spirit and Word
      out of the entire human race,
      from the beginning of the world to its end,
    gathers, protects, and preserves for himself
      a community chosen for eternal life
        and united in true faith.
    And of this community I am and always will be
      a living member.

66. Q. What are sacraments?

  A. Sacraments are holy signs and seals for us to see.
    They were instituted by God so that
      by our use of them
    he might make us understand more clearly
      the promise of the gospel,
    and might put his seal on that promise.

    And this is God's gospel promise:
      to forgive our sins and give us eternal life
        by grace alone
        because of Christ's one sacrifice
        finished on the cross.

Tell how you believe the church can help you grow in faith.

HOLY HABITS

Day 1: Read 1 Corinthians 12:12-13.
How is the church like a body?

Day 2: Read John 4:19-26.
Is there any place or any way that's best to worship God? What does it mean to worship God in spirit and in truth?

Day 3: Read Acts 16:22-34.
What did the jailer's baptism mean to him?

Day 4: Read Luke 22:7-23.
This may have been the first Lord's Supper ever celebrated after Jesus' death and resurrection. What would you have asked Jesus if you were there?

Day 5: Read Revelation 21:1-7.
What do you look forward to in heaven?

PRAYER PATTERNS

Because life can get hectic, you may think you are too busy to pray. But you can always pray "football prayers." Try some this week.

Imagine that Jesus is beside you in every situation that you find yourself: he's on the school bus, in the classroom, on the playing field, in the cafeteria. He's always ready to listen to what you have to say.

Praying to him in busy times is like passing a football when you're out on the field: Jesus will take it and run with it. You don't have to carry it anymore!

So if you notice that your school bus driver is kind of cranky, you could say a quick prayer for the bus driver; if someone says something nasty to you under her breath during class, you can tell God about your hurt feelings, and let go of them. You don't need to fold your hands or bow your head—Jesus is right beside you, listening to your thoughts and words.

Many Christians practice these quick prayers all through the day. Some call them arrow prayers, flash prayers, or javelin prayers. You can call them whatever you like: just be sure to keep sending them along to God.

GOALS

- Discover how some familiar and not-so-familiar "holy habits" can help me grow in my faith
- Identify how these holy habits have helped other people.
- Write specific commitments to help me grow in my practice of holy habits.

I BELIEVE

WHAT ARE HOLY HABITS?

Let's start with the two you've been practicing for the past few weeks: Bible reading and prayer. Later we'll add others that may not be so familiar.

INVENTORY—HOW AM I DOING?

Check all that apply:

1. When it comes to reading the Bible, I
   __ have a regular quiet time set aside for doing that.
   __ really haven't been motivated to work it into my schedule.
   __ read the Bible on kind of an "on-and-off" basis.
   __ would like to be more faithful in my Bible reading.
   __ feel good about my progress in Bible reading.
   __ like using a devotional book or guide to my Bible reading.
   __ have a plan to read through a book or part of a book of the Bible.
   __ other: _____

2. When it comes to praying, I
   __ admit I don't pray very often or regularly.
   __ sometimes pray, sometimes forget to.
   __ try to make prayer part of my daily life.
   __ feel closer to God when I pray.
   __ feel like I'm able to talk to God about whatever's on my mind.
   __ would like to be more faithful in my prayer life.
   __ feel good about my prayer life.
   __ other: _____

3. One way of praying described in this course that I tried and liked is

   _____.

A LIST OF HOLY HABITS

Christians grow spiritually in many ways. We've listed a few below. Put a check by those that you are either doing now or that you might consider doing in the future. Put a question mark by any items that aren't clear to you and that you'd like explained a bit more.

__ **Being Open:** Willingly receiving advice and wisdom from other, more experienced Christians (parents, pastors, teachers, and so on).

__ **Bible Study:** Faithfully reading and studying God's Word, either alone or with other Christians, to learn how God wants you to live.

__ **Celebration:** Expressing some of the joy you feel at being a Christian, usually with other Christians.

__ **Confession:** Examining your conscience, telling God you're sorry, experiencing forgiveness, and determining to live a new life; includes forgiving others for offenses against you.

__ **Fasting:** Going without all or some kinds of food or drink for a short time, for the purpose of concentrating on spiritual things; or abstaining for a time from other practices that are an important part of your life, such as watching TV, shopping, playing computer games, and so on.

__ **Giving:** Contributing some of your money and/or time to help support the church and other ministries.

__ **Living Simply:** Being content with having less so that you can focus on the things in life that really matter.

__ **Meditation:** Spending some time alone quietly thinking about spiritual things, enjoying God's presence, listening to God.

__ **Obedience/Submission:** Putting what Jesus wants you to do ahead of your own will and desires; self-denial.

__ **Prayer:** Bringing your praise, thanks, confession, and needs to God; interceding for others in prayer; being quiet in God's presence, open to his guidance.

__ **Serving:** Giving unselfishly of your time and gifts to help others.

__ **Studying/Learning:** Taking classes at church, reading, trying to learn more about God and living a Christian life.

__ **Witnessing:** Telling or showing others what Jesus means to you.

__ **Worshiping:** Meeting regularly with God's people; responding to God's love with praise and gratitude; being touched by God's Spirit.

WHAT HOLY HABITS CAN DO

Here are a few examples—some unusual, some more ordinary—of what holy habits can do in our lives. Read the examples and talk about what holy habits they illustrate. Look back at the list on pages 66-67 if you wish.

Mama Lupita lives in a poor dusty area of Nuevo Laredo on the Mexican border. She is mother to ninety homeless children. When Lupita heard Jesus' call, she answered with, "Here I am, Lord, send me." Her journey was to her own front door, where she opened her heart and home to a child in need. This was the beginning of what has grown into a large, rambling children's home that provides food, shelter, and much love to unwanted, abandoned, neglected and abused children.

Peter thought he was an expert who had all the right answers when it came to preaching to people who did not know Jesus. But he was in for a surprise. One day, when he was praying and fasting, God showed him he was wrong. Peter learned something new that day, something that changed the world. He learned that God accepted Gentiles (non-Jews) as well as Jews. (For the whole story, read Acts 10:9-48.)

Francis was rich. He had a bright future ahead of him. But one day in a dream, he realized God was calling him to another life. He spent time alone praying and fasting to help him learn God's will. Eventually, he gave away all his wealth and gathered together a band of men whose desire was to reach out to poor people and help them in every way. Today, he is known as Saint Francis of Assisi, author of the well-known prayer "Make me a channel of your peace."

Toyohiko Kagawa became a Christian in his teens after enrolling in a Bible class to learn English. Disowned by his family, he attended a Presbyterian college in Tokyo, then chose a vocation that focused on helping the poor. For many years he lived in a six-foot-square shed in the slums of Kobe. Eventually the Japanese government asked him to supervise social work in Tokyo. He worked hard to improve life for workers in factories and on farms. He established hospitals, schools, and churches, and became a well-known advocate for justice and peace around the world. Toyohiko died in Toyko on April 23, 1960.

Philippe and Joel attend school in Oklahoma. They were surfing the web and learned about James, a boy in Sudan who had been hurt when enemies of

Christianity burned his village. They wanted to help, so they began collecting empty pop cans to raise money for James. Their idea caught on, and now many people are collecting cans for "Kids of Courage." (To learn more, check out www.persecution.com/link/koc.cfm.)

Marie Vogel, an eighth grader from Illinois, heard that a high school youth group had sponsored a child who needed help. She and her family looked up Compassion International online (www.compassion.com) and decided to sponsor a four-year-old boy from the Dominican Republic named Angel Luis. To help raise the $28 a month needed to sponsor their child, Marie and her family give up one normal supper per week, eating a just a bowl of rice or ramen noodles (less than ten cents per serving). The money they would normally spend on groceries goes to sponsor their child. Marie thinks that eating just rice once a week is a cool way to make a big difference in Angel's life. She keeps a picture of him on her locker and all her friends know his name. She looks forward to sponsoring a child on her own someday.

March for Jesus started in England in the 1980s. In May 1987, several Christian groups organized a prayer and praise march through the streets of London. To their surprise, more than 15,000 people turned out in spite of pouring rain. Now the movement has spread around the world with millions of people in more than 130 nations participating each year. The march has expanded its vision and is now called Jesus Day. It's a day when churches not only march and celebrate but also reach out in love with ministry in their cities.

Meredith Brown and a friend head up a before-school prayer group in their big public high school in Wheaton, Illinois. About forty kids attend the twice-weekly meetings—at the unthinkable time of 6:50 to 7:15 a.m.! They spend about half the time singing (guitars and bongos) and half the time praying in groups of four or five. Kids also are invited to share Scripture and say what it means to them. In addition to running the prayer group, Meredith has been sponsoring an eleven-year-old girl from Ecuador for about two years now. She decided to become a sponsor (through Compassion International) after hearing a song called "Do What You Said" by eLi at a Christian concert. This song convinced Meredith she should be helping. She thought, I babysit a lot. I have money. I can do this.

WHAT THE BIBLE SAYS ABOUT HOLY HABITS

A huge cloud of witnesses is all around us. So let us throw off everything that stands in our way. Let us throw off any sin that holds on to us so tightly. Let us keep on running the race marked out for us.

Let us keep looking to Jesus. He is the author of faith. He also makes it perfect. He paid no attention to the shame of the cross. He suffered there because of the joy he was looking forward to. Then he sat down at the right hand of the throne of God.

He put up with attacks from sinners. So think about him. Then you won't get tired. You won't lose hope.

—Hebrews 12:1-3, NIrV

Grow in the grace and knowledge of our Lord and Savior Jesus Christ.

—2 Peter 3:18

Brothers and sisters, God has shown you his mercy. So I am asking you to offer up your bodies to him while you are still alive. Your bodies are a holy sacrifice that is pleasing to God. When you offer your bodies to God, you are worshiping him. Don't live any longer the way this world lives. Let your way of thinking be completely changed. Then you will be able to test what God wants for you. And you will agree that what he wants is right. His plan is good and pleasing and perfect.

—Romans 12:1-2, NIrV

And let us consider how we may spur one another on toward love and good deeds. Let us not give up meeting together, as some are in the habit of doing, but let us encourage one another—and all the more as you see the Day approaching.

—Hebrews 10:24-25

What clues do these passages give you about how to stay on track in your faith journey?

1. Learn from the lives of _____.
2. Get rid of _____.
3. Keep your eyes on the _____.
4. Read and remember the stories in _____.
5. _____ your life to God.
6. Don't just automatically buy in to popular _____.
7. Challenge each other to _____ each other and do _____.
8. _____ together regularly.
9. _____ one another.

Think about some practical ways to do these things in your life. Think about being accountable to others through group Bible study, worship services, classes at church, prayer partners, and so on. Think about prayer, Bible study, keeping a journal, and service to others. Then jot down just a few holy habits that you will try to practice so that you can stay on track and grow spiritually.

HOLY HABITS

BIBLE READINGS FOR THE WEEK

Day 1: Read Mark 1:29-39.
Why would Jesus want to leave the scene of success to be alone? Are you finding time in your own life to be alone with God?

Day 2: Read 1 Corinthians 9:24-27.
What does it take to win a race? What can you learn from this about winning the spiritual race you're running?

Day 3: Read Psalm 119:9-24.
How can reading and reflecting on God's Word help you?

Day 4: Read Matthew 6:5-15.
How do you think God wants you to pray?

Day 5: Read Matthew 6:19-24.
What is your greatest treasure, something you spend a lot of time on?

PRAYER PATTERNS

This week, you may want to try these morning and evening prayers. In the morning, pray this prayer:

Lord, please fill me with your love today. Let your love overflow through me to others. Use my thoughts, words, and deeds to make this day a better day for someone, I pray. Amen.

At the end of the day, ask yourself if God gave you the opportunity to show his love today to someone at school, on the bus, at home, or wherever. Did you take the opportunity?

In your evening prayer, thank God for any opportunities to share God's love that God may have given you. Pray for the person or persons whom you tried to encourage or help in some way. Let the peace of God fill your heart as you end your day.

I BELIEVE . . . I WANT TO BELONG TO THE BODY OF CHRIST

GOALS

- Finish writing a personal creed.
- Learn about the profession of faith process my church will ask me to participate in.
- Reflect on what difference professing my faith will make in my life.
- Commit to using my gifts to participate in the work of the church.
- Talk with my mentor about our relationship.

I BELIEVE

LOOKING BACK

Congratulations! You've reached the last session in this course, and you're getting ready for the rest of your life. Have you enjoyed learning, thinking, and discussing together? What surprised you? What did you find especially helpful or encouraging?

Take a couple of minutes to write down or just discuss your thoughts about this experience. You might want to list some things you'd like to know more about, too, because every Christian should be a growing Christian—exploring, discovering, and changing all the time.

I BELIEVE . . .

Throughout this course you've been writing down your beliefs—about God, Jesus, the Holy Spirit, and so on. Use this page to write a final version of your personal creed. You'll want to look back at what you wrote in sessions 2-7 (look for the "I Believe . . ." heading), but feel free to change or add to your earlier statements, if you wish. Use the blank pages at the end of this notebook if you need more space to write. You may want to share all or part of your written statement with the leaders of your church and with the congregation when you profess your faith.

If you are planning on expressing your faith through song, art, dance, drama, music, and so on, you will want to talk with your mentor about what you have in mind.

I BELIEVE

PROFESSION OF FAITH: HOW DOES IT HAPPEN?

Churches vary on the procedures they follow for profession of faith, so we can't tell you exactly what will happen in your church. But the usual steps go something like this:

■ You tell your pastor, youth pastor, or someone on the church board or council that you would like to make profession of faith.

■ Usually, an elder or other person on your church staff will meet with you to talk about professing your faith.

■ In many churches you are then invited to meet with the church council or board to tell them in person why you would like to take this very important step. This may seem scary—it may feel like you're going to be "grilled" on what you know. You may wonder if you can "fail" this meeting. Actually, this meeting is not about what you know, but about what you believe. So go ahead—tell them! You'll find that the elders and church leaders will be excited and pleased to listen to you. You are an encouragement to adults who have worked and prayed for you. They may have taught you and watched you grow. Now they get to see how God used all their hard work and prayers!

■ Your profession of faith may happen during a regular service or during a special service. For example, some churches schedule professions of faith on Pentecost Sunday, when the church celebrates the coming of the Holy Spirit.

■ In addition to saying "I do" to the questions your pastor asks, you may also be invited to participate in the service in some way—to share your gifts, your "I Believe" statement, or to read the Bible passage or play an instrument.

Here's an example of what happened at one church:

Five kids took the *I Believe* course. Three of them chose to write a creed, one made a banner, and the fifth wrote a song. At the end of the course, they all asked if they could profess their faith. They met with their mentors, the pastor, and other council members at a special meeting. The council members welcomed them and they all sat around a table. Everyone— council members, pastors, mentors and mentees—spent a very wonderful hour talking about their own faith journeys and telling their own stories. The council agreed that all of the kids should publicly profess their faith, and they set a date for the service.

The kids met with the pastor and their mentors later and talked about how each could participate in the service. They decided that one young man would play drums with the worship team, while two kids volunteered to do a puppet show for the children's message. One person's creed became the artwork for the bulletin cover, and one girl sang a solo during the offertory. The written creeds were combined into a single statement which was read by the whole congregation during the service.

After the service, many people congratulated the young people and thanked them for sharing their gifts and their beliefs with everyone.

■ My questions about this process:

■ My ideas on how I can participate and use my gifts during the profession of faith service:

MY PRAYER

Use this space to write a prayer about professing your faith.

▨ What concerns do I need to bring to God about professing my faith? . . .

▨ How do I want God to change my life because of this step I'm taking? . . .

▨ What great plans does God have for my future? . . .

▨ What help do I need from God to live up to my promises? . . .

▨ How can I use my gifts to serve God and my church? . . .

▨ How will I keep growing in faith? . . .

"For I know the plans I have for you," declares the LORD, "plans to prosper you and not to harm you, plans to give you hope and a future. Then you will call upon me and come and pray to me, and I will listen to you. You will seek me and find me when you seek me with all your heart."
—Jeremiah 29:11-13

HOLY HABITS

This week, your readings will focus on blessings and thanksgiving. Your future with God is a shining, wide-open future. Praise God!

Day 1: Read Psalm 98.
What marvelous things has God done for you? How can you thank him?

Day 2: Read Deuteronomy 33:26-29.
These are Moses' words as he blessed Israel before they entered the Promised Land filled with enemies they would have to conquer. Which enemies exist today that will attack your faith? How can this blessing give you hope?

Day 3: Read Numbers 6:22-26.
Write this blessing down, telling in your own words what it means to experience all these promises. (For instance, what would it mean to you that God "keeps you," "makes his face to shine on you," and so on?)

Day 4: Read Hebrews 13:20-21.
What are the "good things" God has equipped you with so you can do his will. Thank God for these blessings.

Day 5: Read Revelation 5:11-14.
When you are singing with all the saints around God's throne, what will you be praising him for?

PRAYER PATTERNS

This week, try "praying the psalms." Many of the psalms were written as personal prayers to God—not just prayers of praise but also prayers expressing the feelings of those who were discouraged, angry, sad, fearful, puzzled, and every other emotion. The saints who wrote these prayers knew that they could talk to God about anything. God delights in listening to his children, no matter how they are feeling or what they're confused about.

Every day this week, pick out one (or part of one) of the psalms that matches your own feelings and offer it as your own morning and evening prayer to God. You may find yourself adding your own words to those of the psalm—that's fine! Or you may decide to write a psalm of your own.

Here are some suggestions:

- Awed by God: Psalm 8
- Gratitude: Psalm 40:1-5; 95:1-7; Psalm 150
- Joy, excitement: Psalm 105:1-5; Psalm 100
- Feeling down: Psalm 86:1-11; Psalm 61:1-4
- Feeling troubled: Psalm 57:1-5; Psalm 73:21-28
- Feeling alone: Psalm 42; 141
- Needing forgiveness: Psalm 32 or 51
- Praying for creation: Psalm 65:9-13; Psalm 19